FLAG ON T

A WOMAN'S GUIDE TO FINDING MR. RIGHT

IN A WORLD FULL OF MR. RIGHT NOWS

FLAG ON THE PLAY

A WOMAN'S GUIDE TO FINDING MR. RIGHT

IN A WORLD FULL OF MR. RIGHT NOWS

DENA REID, ESQ.

WITH

MANDEE BURGESS

www.coderedflag.com

A DIVISION OF LA BELLA ESQ. INDUSTRIES

www.CodeRedFlag.com

Edited by Cassady Fendlay.

Book Cover Designed by Diverse Graphic Designs.

Published by La Bella Esq. Publishing, a division of La Bella Esq. Industries.

1133 Stilford Ave, Plainfield NJ 07060 U.S.A.

ISBN-13: 978-0615960883

ISBN-10: 061596088X:

Printed in the United States of America

Names and identifying characteristics of individuals mentioned have been changed to protect their identities.

This publication is intended to provide authoritative information in regard to the subject matter covered. It is sold with the understanding that the publisher is not engaged in rendering legal, accounting, or other professional advice. If legal or other professional advice is required the services of a competent professional person should be sought.

--From a *Declaration of Principles*

Jointly adopted by the

Committee of the American Bar Association

And a Committee of Publishers and Associations

DEDICATION

This book is dedicated to God who loves us despite ourselves and works all things together for our good. To all of our past loves who have made us the women we are today, and to our family and friends who always show us love and support us.

FOREWORD

by Dena Reid, Esq.

Easter of 2012, I joined a few friends for a dinner party and, as most girlie conversations go, we began talking about men. Not our men, since each of us were single, but the men we had been on dates with over the past few years of our singledom. As we shared horror stories (if there were fairytales we wouldn't still be single now, would we?) one story in particular shocked us all. This guy's first date actions had **RED FLAG** written all over it. As my friend told this story to the group I shouted, "Red flag!" and threw a napkin as if I was an NFL referee. After a few laughs we talked about how great it would be if there was an app that helped warn women of the red flags to look out for in relationships.

A few months later, I met a man that was seemingly normal and gave him my phone number. Not two days later he sent me a lewd message requesting to "lay me on my back and taste me." At that moment I took a photo of the message, created a Facebook community page, and named it Code Red Flag.

CRF has become a community where men and women discuss relationship issues and get feedback from other community members. This book illustrates what I've noticed to be the top 10 recurring **CODE RED FLAGS** that are often overlooked by women (no worries fellas, your book is up next).

My motivation for writing this book is three fold:

1) I've been hurt. Yes me. By not trusting my God-given instincts, or intuition, or whatever you prefer to call it.

2) I am in the healing process, so this is therapeutic for me. The healing process began when I stopped blaming others for my pain and took personal responsibility for allowing people to remain in my life whose intentions were not to bring joy but rather diminish it (be it lovers, friends, or family).

3) I care that you are hurting. Yes I CARE about you! I see too many women who are hurt, bitter, or who have given up on the idea of love. I want to help you by giving you the tools to start on your own journey of healing.

If you have not reached the point where you can trust your own instincts on whether something or someone is a CODE RED FLAG, "Flag On the Play" should be used as a resource book for when you get that feeling that something just ain't right!

About Code Red Flag

When dating #CodeRedFlags pop up everywhere, some we see right away, others we figure out in retrospect. Code Red Flag gives its members the resources to learn whether they should stay and fight for their love or whether it's time to call a "Flag on the Play," run, and cut their losses.

Code Red Flag is a social community that allows its users to interact with other members. Users create a profile on the website, allowing them to post questions to the community and receive responses, ask questions to Dear CRF, read blog posts, and learn about CRF events and so much more. You can also find Code Red Flag on your favorite social media website:

Facebook

www.facebook.com/coderedflag,

Twitter

www.twitter.com/coderedflag,

Instagram

www.instagram.com/coderedflag,

YouTube

www.youtube.com/coderedflag.

DEFINING A CODE RED FLAG:

Noun: a person whose actions illustrate that they may not be what they claim to be.

Adjective: describes a system of words, symbols, actions, or situations that warn of danger and/or a problem.

Verb: in relationships, it is the ability to decode the secret messages behind words, symbols and actions.

TABLE OF CONTENTS

CHAPTER 1

Mr. Hudson River Valley: 'Separated' Means Married

The Hudson River separates New York from New Jersey, but they are both still connected to it. For most women there is a "valley" of sadness surrounding being with a married person. Most women don't want to share a man, they want their own man! But somehow, so many of us get caught up making the excuse, "but he's separated," and believing all the stories (read: lies) about how horrible his wife is.

Ladies, trust me, I speak from experience. When a man tells you he is separated, tell him to take a hike off the George Washington Bridge. He is a CODE RED FLAG up until the day he files for divorce (or preferably until the day the divorce is official because

I've heard some horror stories about spouses who refuse to let go).

There are obvious reasons why married men, and by definition separated men, are Code Red Flags including being disloyal, liars, selfish--just to name a few. Still yet, many women fall into the trap, some unknowingly, others with full and complete knowledge. This is because Mr. Hudson River Valley has perfected the game. He knows women, what we want to see, what we want to hear. He's already gotten a woman to choose to be with him until death should they part.

For one who does not respect his wife, marriage, God, or family, it becomes a game to see how many women he can persuade to choose him. The more he gets chosen, the more he proclaims how good of a man he is. But his perception of what it means to be a good man doesn't fit the definition.

Never confuse a good man with a man who would step out on his wife for a quick thrill with you. And please be sure, 9 times out of 10 that is all you will be to a married man: a temporary fix to fill whichever void he believes his wife is lacking.

Dena's Story:

After graduating from law school, my sister took me to Jamaica as a graduation gift. While there, I met a man who happened to be from my home state. He told my sister and me about how he was divorced and how his wife took everything. We listened compassionately as he bought us drinks. When he got up to leave, he gave me his contact information.

Although I initially had no intention of calling him, I allowed boredom to overtake my better judgment. Surprisingly, our conversations were great. That is until the day I decided to ask him about his relationship status and he replied, "I'm getting a divorce." Insert Confused Face Emoticon and scream it out with me ladies: FLAG ON THE PLAY!!!

Not only was this man still married but he was also a liar. Any wise woman would surely cut her losses and chuck up the deuces at that point, right? Instead, I allowed this man to talk me into believing this was okay. He introduced me to his family, gave me the key to his home, asked me to move in, and so on.

I tried to be comfortable with this situation but I couldn't be. It was like my mind and my feelings were in a constant battle. How could I trust him? He was a married man who had lied to me in the beginning and I had fallen for the bait like a sucker. Our relationship ended in a few short months later and, just as he painted his wife to be such a horrible person, in the end so was I.

I've shared my story to let you ladies know that we have all played the fool. Notice I said we have *played* the fool, not we have been played *for* a fool. I knew better. My gut told me to not go there. My instincts said not to call. But I didn't trust myself. And that is the root cause of the heartache associated with failed relationships: our tendency to overlook the red flags or make excuses for them.

Throughout this guide, we will provide you with scenarios based on anonymous submissions from the Code Red Flag Community. The following scenarios are about dealing with Mr. Hudson River Valley. Take a moment to notice the red flags that you may come across in the story and write them in the space provided after the scenarios before reading our response.

SCENARIO 1

This past August, Brenda met a man whom she absolutely fell for. James was handsome, had a great personality, and he was a leader in his community. He told her his current situation: he is married and his wife is pregnant. He also said that he does not think the baby is his. He plans on making his wife get a DNA test once she delivers the baby.

After a few months, Brenda and James decide to move in together, and his wife lives in a different state. He does not want to file for divorce until his wife "messes up again." James claims his wife has cheated on him in the past, with different guys.

To make Brenda feel better about their "situationship", James has planned a meeting with his family soon, including his wife, which Brenda expects will be a little weird. Brenda has never been in this situation, but he treats her like she has never been treated before. Sexually, financially, and emotionally, he has done things her ex-husband never did. Brenda feels conflicted and needs advice on what to do, but she is too embarrassed to tell any of her friends about her situation she's gotten herself into. She's afraid they will judge her for living with a married man or call her foolish for believing his stories.

Use the space provided on the next page to write down the red flags you spotted:

married / preg wife
doesn't believe the baby's his
DNA test? wife lives in different state
Divorce after wife messes up again
meet family including wife
Not tell friends

Do not worry if you did not see any red flags or maybe only one or two. As you continue to read and reread this book they will become more evident to you. Here are the red flags we saw:

1) She did not have the courage to tell the story. You need to find courage to share stories that are embarrassing, or when you believe that you should have known better. This is one of the ways our intuition speaks to us. It makes us feel uncomfortable in situations that aren't meant for us.

2) She worried about judgment. Many times you will hear people say that "only God can judge them". While it may be true that he is the ultimate judge, others can still judge the situations that we place ourselves in. No matter

how much we attempt to tell ourselves that the judgment of others does not matter, it still bothers us when we are seen in a less-than-favorable light. We want to believe that we are good people who would not willingly place ourselves in positions that portray us in a manner other than how we see ourselves. When we worry whether our actions or the situation we have placed ourselves in will reflect badly on our character, that's our instinct recognizing a red flag situation. The solution is to remove yourself from that situation immediately. Bad company corrupts good character. The relationships you enter and remain in are a direct reflection of your character.

3) She lists surface characteristics like looks while claiming James is a man of character. The

reality is she fell for his swag and swag is not character. Men with charisma are not necessarily men with good character.

This is not to say that all charismatic men lack good character. But swag or charisma, whichever term you prefer, can also be found in players and pimps. We certainly wouldn'list a player or a pimp on an Esquire list of *Men with Good Character*. We must look deeper than the surface level. There must be something that initially attracts us to a man, but that initial attraction should be only the prerequisite to gain your attention.

As we get to know a man, we need to watch his actions to discern whether or not his character matches his swag. When you notice him falling short in areas that a person of good moral character would be held to, it is time to throw him back. Flag on the play! He is no catch.

4) (a) He's married. (b) He says his wife is pregnant and in the next sentence he claims the child is not his. (c) He claims to be waiting on a DNA test to prove this. (d) Even if the baby is not his, he still wants Brenda to wait on the side until his wife "messes up again."

We decided to join each of those red flags into one flaming red flag! The fact that he is married ought to be a red flag of its own. When added to reasons he gives to justify his adulterous affair, it becomes a three alarm fire.

This man has abandoned his wife. His pregnant wife. If he claims that the child is not his, then why does he needs a DNA test? The only possible way James could be certain that the child his wife is carrying is not his is (1) if he stopped having sexual relations with her before the child was conceived or (2) he is incapable of having children. If either of those were the case, he would not need a DNA test to prove he is not the father. This was game.

Now, is it possible that his wife is indeed a cheater? Yes, anything is possible. But why would Brenda want to involve herself in such a messy situation? James is requesting that she be his mistress, his side-chick, until he decides to divorce the woman he vowed to love until death. Think about that. Flag on the play. He is no catch.

5) James speaks badly about his wife to Brenda. You may have heard the saying; those who will talk bad about others *to* you will also talk bad about you. When a man talks bad about a woman to his new love interest, what do you

think his intent is? Nine times out of ten it's to make the new woman sympathize with him, to make her believe that the woman is to blame for the failure of his prior relationship, or, in this case, his current marriage. No relationship is without its issues; the red flag lies in not taking personal responsibility for his part in the demise. Instead, he plays the victim and plays on the new woman's nurturing instinct.

Some women love to believe that they can fix a man's broken heart by loving him and showing him how she is different from the woman who caused his pain. Men know this--and players use it to their advantage. If and when your relationship with such a man gets rocky or ends, the same way he spoke badly about that woman he will surely speak about you. Flag on the play. No catch!

6) Married men who cheat on their wives have a predatory instinct allowing them to scope out vulnerable women to prey on from miles away. Such men often look for someone who is in a weakened state because that person is more likely to accept just about any story they are told. Take note that Brenda feels that he does everything that her ex-husband did not do for her. She is treated like "gold" but there is no ring (actually there is a ring; his wife is wearing it). If James was truly interested in being with Brenda, and cared that much for her, he would divorce his wife. He would have not even approached her for an intimate relationship until the divorce paperwork was filed and he had a legal court document bringing complete closure to his marriage. Brenda probably told him about all of the things that her ex-husband did not do,

so he does exactly what she says her ex was lacking to keep her comfortable in this illicit affair.

7) There are two sides to every story, and the fact that James told her things about his marriage and that she would meet his family soon does not mean that either has or will eventually happen. Regardless, why should she care about meeting the spouse and family when legally the wife still gets everything he has if he were to die. If that child is his, James will discover quickly that it is cheaper to keep his wife and he will likely attempt to make the marriage work for the child.

SCENARIO 2

Amy is madly in love with Brandon, a married man, and has been in a relationship with him for eight years. She knew he was married from the beginning but she felt like there was just something special about him. She says he has treated her like a queen. She never has to ask or want for anything, because he is a great provider.

Recently, his wife of 20 years found out about their relationship and threatened divorce. Brandon immediately ended his affair with Amy and is trying to save his marriage. Amy is distraught and depressed. She wonders how Brandon can profess his love for her for almost a decade and drop her so easily like she never meant anything to him.

Use the space provided on the next page to list the red flags you were able to identify in the above scenario.

Did you spot more red flags with this second scenario? Here are the ones we noticed:

1) Signing up to be a side chick, mistress, other woman or whatever you want to call it is never wise. Though there are some men who leave their wife and marry their former lover that is the exception, not the rule! Amy thought that her years in would make her an exception. In love there are no guarantees, especially when you're a willing member of a love triangle.

2) Amy carried on an illicit love affair with a man who was being deceitful to the woman he vowed to love, honor, and cherish for the rest of his life, but somehow thought the throne belonged to her. She tricked herself into believing she was being treated as a queen when she was nothing

more than a paramour. The things he bought her in exchange for her honor were nothing more than frivolous material items he could quickly walk away from, unlike the life he made with his wife.

3) Amy is confused about what love is. Brandon carrying on an 8 year affair with her is not about love. His cheating on his wife was not love. It was pure unadulterated lust and selfishness. This is the epitome of a man wanting his cake and eating it too. Amy was just as selfish. She attempted to receive blessings and joy from the wife's pain. Now that it has backfired on her, which eventually happens with such affairs, she feels pain and wants to blame him for lying to her for the last eight years. However, she should not ignore the fact that she was a willing

participant in this man's web of deceit the entire time.

4) If a man is willing to cheat on his wife for eight years, why would he not cheat on you if he was to be in a relationship with you? Again, it is cheaper to keep his wife. After twenty years of marriage, his wife may be entitled to half of the marital assets and collect an alimony check monthly.

Infidelity affects children, spouses and the mistress in similar ways. The child of an unfaithful spouse will likely have trust issues when it comes to relationships. They may also experience confusion in regards to identifying real love. They likely will question why a person who supposedly loves them and their mother can be so unfaithful and cause so much pain.

The spouse who was cheated on will likely have a hard time maintaining the current marriage or may be reluctant to start over again. The mistress often begins having trust issues and may suffer from guilt when she tries to move on to a healthier relationship with a man of her own.

Too many women believe that they are the ones who will make a cheater change his game. Those women often end up bitter and are unable to trust a good man if and when they meet one. Don't be that woman. When you meet a married man and he tries to pursue you, cut him short, yell Code Red Flag! FLAG ON THE PLAY! And save yourself from the inevitable heartache.

CHAPTER 2

Mr. Burger King: He Likes It His Way

Mr. Burger King is also known as "Mr. Have It My Way." He has convinced himself that he is entitled to having women any way he wants to have them and treats them as his personal toy. He may say things like, "I wish I had something sexy lying next to me right now," and he expects a woman to jump at the opportunity. This man is often very popular, and has money and/or political pull (or at least he tells himself that he does). This man likely has a series of failed short term relationships and/or multiple children by multiple women. He is likely to be indiscriminate with where he places his seed so he does not bother with using protection.

Mandee's Story:

One of the most eye opening experiences of my adult life was when I was asked to be a man's "main" lady. He told me that he was incapable of being with one woman and wanted me to be the main one to reap the benefits of his time and money. Of course, my answer was an emphatic NO! I feel that I carry myself as a lady, so I asked him why he would even think to approach me in such a manner. He said that he was drawn to the way I carry myself and he "just wanted to be honest."

He explained that most men would just cheat and hope to not get caught. He said that he wanted me to know that the other women would only get sex, no quality time. I reminded him that neither he nor I can control human behavior.

Aside from the potential health risks involved (condoms are not 100%, and oral sex transmits disease), a woman who agrees to be the side chick has issues. Someone who is willing to accept a piece of a man is usually hoping that he will eventually want her to be his "main" lady.

There are some women who strictly want sex with no strings attached, but those women are the exception, not the rule. If a woman is being a mistress in hopes that she will become the main woman, and she does not get what she wants, that could become a fatal attraction. Who knows what such a woman could be capable of?

No more than a month later he informed me that he decided to be in an exclusive relationship with a woman he had been seeing on and off for a year. Ladies, he did not miraculously come to his senses and decide that he can now be a one woman man. He knew all along that he had a main woman already. He wanted to see what I would accept.

Remember, a man can only do to you what you allow him to do. Had I accepted being one of the many, he would have done just that. There may have come a time when he left me for the side chick who he had been seeing on and off for the year. Ladies, you have a choice as to whether to fall victim or not.

Ladies, a true king takes his time when selecting a mate, let alone the mother of his children. He will study her from afar, so that he is as respectful as possible when he does approach. He will know some things that she likes so that his first approach will leave a lasting impression.

During the getting-to-know-her phase, he will observe her words and, more importantly, her actions. He will look at how she makes decisions and how she handles adversity. A king does this because he needs a queen to help him raise his future prince and/or princess.

The Burger King, on the other hand, will fall head over heels in lust with outward appearances. The relationship will blast off like a rocket only to crash and burn, possibly leaving a baby in the wake of the crash.

Ladies, stop settling for Mr. Burger King when you can have a real king treating you as a queen should be treated. Mr. Burger King may know how women tick; he is likely very skilled in the bedroom and he preys on women he sees as weaker vessels. If you should come across a Mr. Burger King, don't place an order. Throw your flag on his plays.

The follow scenarios are about dealing with Mr. Burger King. When you identify the red flags, write them in the space provided after the scenario and then read our response.

SCENARIO 1

Marisa just ended a three year relationship with the
man she believed was her soul mate, after finding out
he had been cheating on her for the entirety of their
relationship. Furious, Marisa has decided that she will
date Marcus, the cutie pie that lives in the apartment
next door to her ex.

Marcus has a girlfriend whom he has been with for a
year, but he tells Marisa that his girlfriend is not her
concern. Since she wants to get back at her ex and
have a warm body next to her at night, Marisa agrees
to Marcus' terms.

After a few weeks of this friends-with-benefits
relationship, Marisa begins to fall for Marcus. She asks
Marcus how he feels about her and he answers, "I
think you're cool. I really enjoy spending time with

you and the sex is amazing." Marisa takes that answer for now and begins to plot on how she can make Marcus hers exclusively.

One day, Marisa gets a phone call from her friend Diane. Diane says she's in a local bar and just saw Marcus come in with a girl who is not the girlfriend Marisa knows about. Marisa immediately heads to the bar to see for herself. When Marcus sees her, he completely ignores her presence. This infuriates Marisa so she causes a scene. Marcus yells at her "You're crazy, you're not my woman. You know what it is. My girl would never cause a scene like this. And you could never be my girl acting like this."

Marisa runs out the bar in tears, feeling used. She says she doesn't understand where this all went wrong.

Use the space provided on the next page to list the red flags you were able to identify in the above scenario.

Here are the red flags we found:

1) Marisa did not give herself time to heal from the failed relationship with her ex. Marisa was in an emotionally weakened state and the attention and sex escalated her emotions. Marcus was crystal clear about his intentions, but in her mind she tried to make it more than it was. For all she knows, Marcus may have told her ex that he was "smashing" her. That may be a game that both of them play.

2) Marisa signed up knowing the terms of their 'situationship' but failed to play her position. She had no commitment and thus had no say in who Marcus could spend his time with. She was dead wrong for plotting to get him away from his girlfriend and made herself look ridiculous for

trying to embarrass him in public when he was with another woman. Marcus was honest about the fact that he had no feelings for her and she agreed to do it his way. She set herself up for failure from the beginning.

3) When Marcus sees her, he completely ignores her presence. Many men would get nervous, but this is his modus operandi (aka his M.O.). Marcus sees himself as honest Abe, so he believes he can treat women as he pleases and his game is not to be disrupted.

4) Marcus yells at her, "My girl would never cause a scene like this. And you could never be my girl acting like this." This statement is indicative that Marcus may have an arrangement with his current girlfriend. If his girlfriend lives in the

same town, he is not worried about being seen out with another female because he knows that his girlfriend will "behave" herself, as he has taught her, if she sees him out and about with other women.

SCENARIO 2

Ronda met Richard when they attended college together for their undergraduate studies. They lived in the same dormitory, right across the hall from each other. Quickly they became good friends, studying, working out, and hanging out together. Her friends became his friends and vice versa.

One night, Richard decides they should take their relationship to the next level. Out of nowhere, he straddles Ronda as she sits on his couch and begins kissing her. Shocked, Ronda makes up an excuse to leave and then does her best to avoid Richard.

A few weeks later he calls, telling her he misses her and asking why she's been avoiding him. She tells him that she sees him as a friend and would prefer to keep it that way. He explains to her that friends make the best lovers but he will respect her wishes. They continue their friendship like the episode on his couch never happened.

Shortly before graduation, Ronda begins to think that maybe she wants to see if she and Richard would be good as more than just friends. She tells him she's willing to try and he is ecstatic. Once they have sex, everything changes. He begins talking down to her, being disrespectful, and openly flirting with other women in front of her.

Each time he acted this way, Ronda would call it off, but Richard always found a way to fix it and get her to come back to him. They continued to have dates and have sex, sometimes without a condom, and Ronda gets pregnant. When she tells Richard, he becomes infuriated and begins to beat her. He demands that she get an abortion and she does.

Ronda doesn't understand how her loving friend became such a monster.

What red flags do you see in this scenario? Use the space provided on the next page to list them.

Here are the red flags we caught:

1) "One night Richard decides they should take their relationship to the next level. Out of nowhere, he straddles Ronda as she sits on his couch and begins kissing her." This is an example of controlling and aggressive behavior. If he was truly her good friend, he would have shown the respect of discussing the relationship and would make the decision to take the relationship to the next level with her consent. Instead, he neglects her feelings and makes the assumption that she must want him to.

2) It takes weeks for Richard to contact Ronda and they continue the friendship as if nothing happened. A friend would have immediately apologized and wanted to talk to Ronda to

smooth things over and gain some clarity on why she is upset.

3) With the two red flags above, if Ronda was thinking clearly, she would have graduated and kept her friendship with Richard intact. Instead, she offers him an intimate relationship. Richard is ecstatic because he was keeping her around as a friend with the possibility of having sex one day, and this was his opportunity to achieve that goal. This is why everything changed after sex.

4) Richard become emotionally and verbally abusive when he begins talking down to her, being disrespectful, and openly flirting with other women in front of her: yet another red flag that Richard is abusive.

5) Ronda ignored all of the signs of abusive behavior. When Richard finally puts his hands on

her, Ronda claims she "doesn't understand how her loving friend became such a monster." He was a monster all along; she just decided to ignore the signs. Once she gave in and shared[i] her body with him, he began to fully unleash that abusive side.

CHAPTER 3

Mr. Rolling Stone:

Multiple Children with Different Women

In 1972, the rhythm and blues group The Temptations released the song, "Papa Was a Rolling Stone." The chorus spoke about a man who was a lover of many women, all of whom he left with children as he continued his prowl onto the next unsuspecting woman. Additionally, the verses speak about a man who abandoned his wife and children only later to be found out to have made another woman his wife and made a family with her as well.

A rolling stone is defined as a person who refuses to settle down in one place for any substantial time. Does this type of man sound like a good catch? Of course not. But many women, knowingly and unknowingly, become entangled with a man who has a history of moving from one woman to the next and planting his seed in each one without being responsible for his progeny.

Why do some women allow themselves to get caught up in such situations? There are as many reasons as there are rolling stones. Many women fall for the myth that once a woman has reached a certain age, normally, 30 or older, the likelihood of finding a mate without a child is slim to none. However, let us remember the biblical character Sarah. Sarah was Abraham's wife. God had promised Abraham that he would be the father of nations. Yet Sarah believed she could not conceive a child so she gave Abraham permission to lay with her hand maiden, with whom he had his first child.

See like many women, Sarah lost faith. Her lack of faith led her to make a decision that went against the will of God. Sarah believed that she was too old to bear a child for Abraham. But God doesn't deal in the impossible. He is a deliverer of the possible. As he promised, Sarah became pregnant with a son.

As women, we play the role of faithless Sarah when we allow society's time pressures to direct our paths, instead of the will of God, and we settle for a man who is not the one chosen for us. Then, when that man rolls on, we give up on love, and, in turn, giving up on God. Remember ladies, a man who won't commit to his family is no catch.

Another issue is that it is now socially expected and accepted that by the age of 30 most, if not all, men will have at least one child, whether out of wedlock or from a previous marriage. In fact, I've heard some women say that they give a side eye to any man over 40 who has never been married or in a serious committed relationship. It would seem to be a double edged sword. On one hand, we worry about a man's willingness to commit and we judge that by his former relationships. On the other hand, we don't want a man who over-commits his body and lays wildly across the playing field. But both those examples are extremes. There is a happy medium that can be found without having to feel as we need to settle for Mr. Rolling Stone or Mr. Bellevue (the man who is afraid of commitment).

Read these next scenarios about Mr. Rolling Stone and write the red flags you find in the space provided after the scenario.

Scenario 1

Danielle met Paul six months ago at a dinner party at a mutual friend's home. Not only was Paul incredibly good looking, but he had a way with words and the charisma of a Barack Obama or John F. Kennedy. Danielle and Paul flirted all night and she says that he only had eyes for her that night. They exchanged numbers and began talking and texting throughout the day until he finally asked her out on a dinner date. They began dating, she believes exclusively, and soon became intimate.

The day before their six month anniversary, Danielle gets a phone call at work. It's Paul's ex-wife Lisa causing drama. Lisa tells Danielle that Paul is her first, the father of her three children, and that she still sleeps with Paul. She also informs Danielle that she is Paul's high school sweetheart and she has seen many others come, have children with him, and go, but she remains the constant woman in his life and will always be the one he comes back to.

After hanging up on Lisa, Danielle calls Paul to let him know about the crazy claims made by his alleged ex-wife. Paul becomes defensive and tells Danielle to just hang up the phone the next time Lisa calls. Later that night, Paul tells Danielle that he has five children with three different women. Danielle thinks this is a red flag.

Use the space provided on the next page to write down the red flags you identified.

Here are the red flags that jumped out for us:

1) Danielle has been with this man for half of a year and not once has he mentioned to her that he was previously married. That is not a slight. That is what is considered a lie by omission. Some people like to believe that a lie only occurs when one is asked a question and responds untruthfully. I disagree. Intentionally omitting relevant information is also a deception.

2) In addition to him omitting that he was once married, Paul conveniently left out the fact that he has any children. Finding out from another woman, who happens to be his ex-wife and mother of three of his children, that he has fathered five children with multiple women

should tell her to throw the flag on this player's game. He is not a catch!

3) After receiving this information, Danielle does as most women would: she calls her man to find out the truth. Paul is given the opportunity to come clean but instead he attempts to play the old Jedi mind trick on her and becomes defensive. When a man is in the wrong, a man of good character will do all within his power to correct the situation, because he knows he is not perfect. A man of bad character will try to reverse the situation and play the role of the victim. The latter type of man is no catch, throw the red flag and get yourself out of that situation.

4) Danielle "believes" that they are dating exclusively. Never assume anything until a man

tells you that he wants to be in an exclusive relationship. She became intimate with him soon after that. Some men will bank on the woman assuming that they are in an exclusive relationship to make the woman more comfortable with having sex. Know where you stand in a relationship before you decide to lay down.

5) What Lisa said is a red flag in itself. She basically said that she is okay with "waiting on the bench" for Paul and takes pride in being his fall back. When the relationship is over, both people need to have the courage to either be alone or move on completely. Paul may just be having sex with Lisa, but either way she will create problems by being a part of his personal life in any capacity. The only interaction they should have is for the children, period. Even if

she is lying about the sex, this situation should be avoided. Paul obviously does not have their relationship in check and she refuses to let go because he was "her first and high school sweetheart."

6) Having children with his ex-wife is one thing, but having two other children with different women is an indication that Paul is careless with his seed and does not make very thoughtful decisions in regard to relationships. Hence, the fact that Paul and Danielle rushed into what in reality is a "situationship" means that Danielle could easily become baby mama number four. She will be if she falls for Paul's tricks and tries to trap him to spite Lisa. That would certainly backfire and she would be another casualty of Paul's game. Paul may have charisma similar to

Obama, but he is clearly no commander-in-chief.

SCENARIO 2

Thalia is a beautiful, educated, and single 35 year old woman with no children. She dates regularly but has not been in a relationship for over three years. She's fed up and worried that if she waits much longer, her chances of starting a family will be little to none. She decided to try something new with online dating sites. Most of the men that message her are not her type but one really catches her eye. Damon is 38 and his profile says he is educated, never married, and is childless as well; however, he states he is interested [i] in having children someday with the right woman.

They message for a few days and Thalia finally agrees to give Damon her number. During their first conversation she hears children playing in the background. Damon says that his sister and her children are staying with him because she was recently laid off.

They start dating and Thalia falls heads over heels with Damon. After two years of dating, Thalia becomes pregnant. Soon after, Thalia begins to wonder why she has never been to Damon's home nor has she met his sister and her children. Suspicious, Thalia learns Damon's address and decides to surprise him one day.

When she knocks on the door a little boy answers. She asks for Damon and the little boy screams, "Daddy there is some lady at the door for you." When Damon comes to the door and sees her, he immediately slams the door in her face. She has not heard from him since, he has not answered her calls and he has closed his social media accounts. Thalia is hurt and feels as though Damon has played her.

Can you identify the red flags she missed? Use the space provided on the next page to list them.

Here are the red flags we caught:

1) If you haven't met any of your significant other's family members, an eyebrow should be raised (unless, of course, he is an only child whose parents are both deceased and those parents were also only children with both parents deceased). There should be an auntie, cousin, grandparent or *someone* who has crossed your path in two year's time. While Thanksgiving and Christmas are major family holidays that not every significant other will be invited to immediately, there are surely other events such as cook-outs, birthdays, weddings, baby showers, etc., that grant an opportunity for an invite. The red flag here is: why is he hiding you or what is he hiding from you?

2) An even bigger red flag is that Thalia has never been to Damon's home in two years. This should have raised some suspicion, or at the very least piqued her curiosity. Now, I understand that some people aren't comfortable with bringing people they just met to their home. But once sexual intercourse has been added to the relationship then the comfort level should be raised to the point where home visits, especially overnight visits, would be welcomed.

3) Another cause for an eyebrow raiser is that she felt the need to go snooping. The instinct that caused her to snoop was the red flag flying high.

Although Thalia is a beautiful, educated, and single, she falls for Mr. Rolling Stone's game because her self-esteem is not where it should be and she does not know her self-worth. After three years without a relationship, Thalia becomes worried that if she waits much longer, her chances of starting a family will be little to none. There is no reason why a beautiful and educated woman cannot begin a family. It may not be on her time schedule, but God is always right on time. It is better for her to remain single, work on loving and building herself up before getting into a relationship with another broken person.

When you allow God to put you back together, you become whole again. If you attempt to superglue yourself back together, then you become damaged goods. You will end up putting yourself on clearance because of the defects and the broken man buying is just looking for something cheap regardless of the condition.

When you are whole, you will be in the section of the store where valuable items are placed. Only the most prosperous (not just financially) men would dare venture into that section because the work they have allowed God to put in has made them able to afford a woman of your quality.

Now please don't mistake this chapter to mean that men with children are all red flags. There are reasons why a man would no longer be with the mother of his child. She could be deceased. She could have been abusive (yes, women can be abusers as well). It is also likely that she displayed red flags herself.

There are numerous men who are single parents because they have fallen for and had children with women who were not mentally, emotionally, or spiritually able to be a good wife or mother. These men are not to be counted out because of this. I do, however, suggest that you allow a man who has been in this situation time to heal before moving forward with a relationship and perhaps keep him at a safe distance (i.e. don't sleep with him and catch feelings) while you try to figure out what's really going on.

CHAPTER 4

Mr. Bellevue: Don't Commit Me

Bellevue is a well-known hospital located in Manhattan, New York, infamous for its psychiatric ward. The name Bellevue is now used as a synonym for crazy. Not the fun kind of crazy, as in college kids on a weekend night, but the examined and committed in a mental institution type of crazy. As such, Mr. Bellevue is the kind of man that believes being tied down to one woman equates to being locked down in a mental institution.

Many women have written in to Code Red Flag asking what it means when the guy she has been seeing exclusively tells her that he's just not ready for a relationship. Some men avoid commitment to a woman as if they were avoiding commitment to a mental institution. Many times these women have started dishing out girlfriend or wife benefits, including but not limited showing "her man" (in her mind only) her special bedroom tricks. Ladies, when a man says he isn't ready for a relationship, believe him. This is not a challenge that you should eagerly accept. No matter how many hoops you jump through or how many special tricks you believe you have, a man is not going to commit to a woman until he finds that one he wants to commit to. Only he can make that decision. You can't make it for him.

We've heard many women and men talk about the 'boyfriend experience'. Think of it as a Jedi mind trick. You get the benefits of a boyfriend, i.e. quality time, gifts, sex, but not the commitment. Some may ask, 'so what's so wrong with that?' The problem is while you're pretending to be in a relationship with Mr.

Bellevue, you're missing out on the man that would happily want to be committed to you and only you. For whatever reason, Mr. Bellevue is not ready for a mature relationship. Until he accepts the fact that he is as ready today as he will be tomorrow, he is stuck in the never ending quest of getting "ready." Don't be stuck with him. Notice the red flag and keep it moving. Please know there is a difference between being patient and wasting your time. The actions of the other person should help you discern which is which. It's been said numerous times, "no matter how good a woman is, she's never good enough for a man who is not ready."

Dena's story:

Since I've been celibate, I've had numerous men attempt to be the one to make me rethink my vow. One such guy told me that, although he couldn't commit to me at this time, he promised to give me a better experience than any man I had ever been with. He offered international trips, to help pay my student loans and bills, even his "hurricane tongue." I could have everything and anything I wanted-- but not a commitment. I routinely turned down his advances, but every time I said no he would try to enrich his offer with more luxurious gifts.

When I wouldn't accept his gifts, he then attempted to make me jealous by telling me about all he was doing for the other women he was seeing. His planned backfired on him horribly. The more he told me about his escapades with other women, the more turned off I became. He finally gave up once I sat him down and explained to him that I thought he was nasty.

See, over three months or so, he had told me stories about at least four different women, all of whom he had introduced to this "hurricane tongue" of his. I told him that even had I not been celibate, I was not and never will be attracted to a man as loose as him.

Scenario 1

Donna has been "talking" to Howard for seven months now. She says everything has been great between them. In the beginning, they decided to be cautious with their hearts and just keep things light and fun. Now, with the holidays approaching, Howard has started acting weird. Donna wanted to give him a gift and he refused, saying he "doesn't want to feel trapped." Howard says he needs some space and wants to take a few days off. When they talk about the future, he has no idea of what he wants. Howard always replies that he wants to take it a day at a time. He believes that plans are too stressful because you never know what will happen. Donna's feelings are hurt and she thinks he is stringing her along. She wants to give up on him and move on but he sucks her back in every time. She thinks he may be playing games and keeping her as his back-up plan.

Use the space provided on the next page to write down the red flags you spotted.

We noticed the following red flags:

1) Neither one of them seems to be emotionally available. Love and relationships involve risk. There is nothing wrong with taking things slow so that you can get to know each other, but purposely holding back emotions will hinder the natural progression of the relationship.

2) As the holiday got closer, Howard started acting weird and he wouldn't accept Donna's gift. Why would a gift make someone feel trapped? This indicates that he really had no intentions on being in a committed relationship with Donna but she has made it easy up until this point. Giving gifts is something people do in a real relationship.

3) The fact that he needed a few days off may be a signal that he is spending the holiday with someone who he truly wants to be with. That person may be giving him the cold shoulder, and Donna is his place filler.

4) When Donna and Howard talk about the future, he has no idea of what he wants and always replies that he wants to take it a day at a time. He believes that plans are too stressful because you never know. No one needs an indecisive man as the head of their household. That statement is a flaming red flag. A man who is ready to settle down knows what he wants and will not waste time with someone who does not fit the bill.

Donna is being strung along, possibly for sex and/or companionship. Howard is saying in one breath that he doesn't know what he wants and then in the next he is sucking her back into the 'situationship'. This is a game to keep her as his back-up plan. Howard is clearly not ready to settle down, but Donna will do for the time being.

Scenario 2

Sandra has been in what she believed was an exclusive relationship with Scott for two years. Their relationship was often long distance because she was away at school. Although he only came to visit her at college once, she was okay with it since it was a four hour drive from where he lived. She invited him to her graduation but he had an excuse for why he could not make it.

After graduation, she moved back to her home state in a town not too far away from Scott. He was taking the summer to finish a research paper for his Master's degree and asked Sandra for her help. She agreed and did the majority of the research and edited his paper for him. When he received his grade, he told her and she replied that he had the best girlfriend in the world. He responded by letting her know that he did not have a girlfriend. Sandra was stunned and immediately cut all communication with him. She wrote in to the Code Red Flag community because she does not understand how he could say that to her. After all, for the last two years they have done everything that a couple does, including sex. She is hurt and confused.

Can you find the red flags Sandra missed? Write them in the space provided on the next page.

Here are the red flags we were able to identify:

1) Sandra had been in what she "believed" was an exclusive relationship. Never assume anything. A man can treat you like a companion and it may resemble a relationship. Hence the fact that they "did everything that a couple does, including sex." This did not constitute a relationship. This is a classic case of the guy who is having his cake and eating it too. He was probably spending time with a female in his home town (which is why he was not pressed to travel to see her.) Scott may not have intended for the local female to take Sandra's place initially, but she obviously did. Sandra and Scott should have discussed their relationship status openly, rather than making assumptions.

2) In a two year time frame, Scott only came to visit Sandra at college once. A man that wants to be with you will put in whatever effort is necessary to spend time with you and grow the relationship. Even if there are other factors like lack of finances involved, where there is a will there is a way to go see your woman more than once in two years.

3) Sandra invited Scott to her graduation but he made up an excuse for why he could not make it. Scott made a strategic move. As with not making the effort to travel to see Sandra at school, actions speak louder than words. Not taking the time to support Sandra during a major milestone in her life says, "I am not your man and I do not want to even give you the impression that this is going any further."

4) Sandra is obviously a really nice person, and Scott has taken her kindness for granted. He probably knew that Sandra thought they were more than friends and used that to his advantage when he asked her to help with his paper. If Sandra had paid closer attention to his actions, she could have initiated a conversation with him and possibly gotten to the bottom of things sooner rather than later.

CHAPTER 5

Mr. Cliff Jumper: Sexing is Not Dating

Even if a man's name is Cliff, you don't have to be his jump off, booty call, friend with benefits, etc. More than likely, he will not provide you with a parachute or a safety net to catch you and you will hit rock bottom. If the man you're interested in does not show interest in you other than sex, then ladies that is a Code Red Flag. It's time for you to throw that flag on the play and retrieve your dignity.

Often times women believe that if they know how to please a man, including sexually, he will be hers forever. But the reality is many women have wasted years, energy and effort auditioning to be some man's wife, giving him all the benefits thereof, yet he never comes around.

The reason he never comes around is because he never intended you to play the role of his wife. Just as women often put some men in the friend zone, there are times when men put women in the "for entertainment purposes only" zone. He will keep you around and reap the benefits you're providing because he can; because you allow him. Only you can decide that you don't want to jump off that cliff without a parachute. Only you can decide that you are worth more than sex. You make that decision by not discounting yourself to be any man's jump off.

Remember, no matter how good a woman thinks she is, she will never be good enough for the man who is not ready. And she can't make him ready. He will be ready in his own time. Life is too short to hang off the cliff waiting for him to be ready. You can and must do better.

The following scenarios illustrate some red flags that are associated with dating a man like Mr. Cliff Jumper. Read them and use the space provided after the scenario to write the red flags you spot.

SCENARIO 1

Tasha met Robert through a mutual friend and was instantly physically attracted to him. She was pleasantly surprised that he was also funny and had a great personality. Tasha and Robert began to get to know each other, but most of their interactions were over text. Tasha met Robert at a party that he and his boys were throwing, so she knew that he hung out quite a bit. When she would ask him to take her out, Robert always used his two children or lack of finances as an excuse as to why he could not go out, yet he would club whenever he wanted to. They barely talked unless Tasha initiated the contact.

When Robert initiated contact it would be a "hey you" text, followed by "come over I want to see you." If Tasha happened to be on her menstrual cycle, the texting conversation would end abruptly. Tasha wasn't totally feeling the fact that they didn't go out much, but the sex was incredible and she says they had so much fun together. The majority of the time Tasha would go to Robert's house late at night and leave in the morning, so they never had breakfast or dinner together. Whenever Tasha wanted to talk about a relationship, Robert would change the subject.

When Tasha had not heard from Robert in a couple of weeks, which was not like him, she logged into Facebook and saw that Robert had changed his relationship status and was now in a relationship. Tasha was devastated. About a month later, Robert sent an "I miss you text" to Tasha. Tasha fussed at him and he apologized. He said that he had a weak moment and made the mistake of trying to have a relationship with his now ex. Tasha had been without sex for a while and needed some, so she went over Robert's house.

Tasha knows that she began having sex with no commitment, but she really loves spending time with him and feels like they have a connection. She is not sure as to whether she should proceed with the relationship being that she wants more.

What red flags did you find? Use the space provided on the next page to list the red flags you found.

We recognized these red flags:

1) As adults, we should not be getting to know each other via text. We are not saying that you have to stay on the phone all night like teenagers, but a man should put some effort in to call more than he texts. Technology is supposed to work for you, not against you. A lot can be lost in the translation of a text message, especially if you don't know the person well.

2) When Tasha would ask Robert to take her out, he always had an excuse, yet he would club without her. If a man shows you that he can make an effort to do what he wants to do, except when it comes to you, you need to throw the red flag.

3) They barely talked unless Tasha initiated contact. When Robert initiated contact it would be an invitation for sex. If she was unable to perform, the texting conversation would end abruptly. This is clearly a man who is only interested in a sexual relationship. He is not even putting forth effort to get to know you as a friend. This does not mean that you are not attractive enough or don't have enough to offer to make him want to be in a relationship. This means that he is too lazy to put in the effort. It is a clear indication that he is not ready for a serious relationship. It is possible that he has been single for so long that he has gotten complacent.

4) Whenever Tasha wanted to talk about a relationship, Robert would change the subject.

The more Tasha allowed this, the more Robert played this game.

5) When Tasha took Robert back, after actually committing to a relationship with someone else and making it public, that was like a wake up slap to the face. If that man is ignoring the relationship conversation with you, and shortly after that is in a relationship that should tell you all you need to know: he does not want a relationship with you. He's not your catch.

SCENARIO 2

Alexis met Chris online. They had great conversations on the phone, and Chris seemed to be family-oriented. Chris said that he wanted to take things slow and court her so that she would know that he was not just trying to have sex with her. He also said that he liked her very much and could see himself being with her long term. Yet Chris was not very reliable and would cancel dates at the last minute with very little explanation. They managed to go on only one date in a very remote location that Chris chose.

Alexis began to notice that Chris would talk to her up until he arrived in the garage of his home, then he would get off of the phone saying it was due to a poor signal inside of his house.

Most times, Chris was not available until very late at night on the weekends, but Alexis was trying to be understanding of the fact that Chris was working a lot. He would then go to her house and they'd have sex. He always left immediately after.

Alexis likes Chris but is not satisfied with how their relationship is going.

Use the space provided on the next page to list the red flags you were able to identify in the above scenario.

The following are the red flags we found:

1) Chris was not very reliable and would cancel dates at the last minute with very little explanation. There are circumstances that will force someone to reschedule. However, if it becomes a recurring theme, then there could be a problem that needs to be addressed.

2) They managed to go on only one date in a very remote location that Chris chose. If there are restrictions on where you can be seen with him, that is a problem. Even if the person is not married, if they have to hide you from an ex, they are not over it. If the person is hiding you from other sex partners, that is a problem too.

3) Chris not being able to talk in the house should cause an eyebrow to rise. Most people will get a

carrier that they can use in the house or have a house phone for emergency purposes. If a man is truly single, there should be no restrictions on when or where he can speak with you. Chris was also not available on the weekends until late night. There is a line of reasoning that says the simplest explanation is usually correct, and the simplest explanation for these behaviors is that Chris has another woman in the house.

CHAPTER 6

Mr. Hide and Seek

Mr. Hide and Seek is the man who keeps his distance because he does not want to connect emotionally. He may disappear for days, weeks, or even months at a time with no contact at all. Then, once you've finally put him out of your mind, you get a text from him claiming to miss you or something similar as he tries to feel you out. His only explanation for dropping off the face of the earth is that he is extremely busy at work or school.

Susan Walsh, author of *Hooking Up: Sex, Dating, and Relationships on Campus*, writes on her blog, *Hooking Up Smart,* three possible reasons a man might behave this way:

> 1. He is immature;

2. He is transient. (Often related to #1);

3. He is emotionally dysfunctional.

Ms. Walsh guides us on the "most important criterion in selecting a partner . . . his enthusiasm for getting into a relationship." If he is playing hide and seek, recognize the need to call a flag on the play and end the games before you find yourself deep in the penalty zone.

Mandee's Story:

I had a guy friend who was very much like Mr. Hide and Seek. We had contemplated dating, but he was fresh out of a divorce and just wanted to play the field. I knew that I would want more, so instead of trying to change him, I placed myself in the friend zone.

We became really good friends and counseled each other through numerous relationships over the years. During this time we confided in each other and our children became friends. My mother grew to love him and co-workers could not understand why I wasn't trying to be with a handsome and successful man.

As a result of us becoming close, I began to see what poor choices he made in regard to relationships. I could also see that he had a real problem connecting on an emotional level. One minute he would be fully involved with a woman, then, out of the blue, he would be distant and could not be reached.

During these times he may or may not respond to text messages from the woman he was dating, although he preferred to text because he felt that he could "keep his distance and control the conversation."

The entire time we were friends, I could feel the sexual tension, and he would always act a little jealous when we discussed people I was dating. During a vulnerable time (I was fresh out of a relationship), he was consoling me and we cuddled. I started to think it could be something because we cared so much for each other. We discussed the fact that I could not handle being his jump off (aka friend with benefits) and that if we were to ever become involved sexually, I would want a commitment.

The mistake I made was thinking that he would be emotionally different with me than he had been with any other female. When a man shows you who he is, you better believe him. The day that we agreed to make an attempt at a relationship, he saw a post that I shared from the Code Red Flag Facebook page and messaged me because he thought that I was trying to send him a "subliminal message".

Last time I checked, I am a grown woman with three children and a career, part of which involves me sharing posts from

Code Red Flag. I assured him that if I wanted to tell him something, I would come directly to him. Needless to say, he got scared and retreated as he had done so many times before with other women.

There is beauty in really getting to know someone before making a commitment to be exclusive. The biggest mistake women make is thinking that our personality will transfer to another person, or that someone will miraculously change their ways by virtue of being with us. Every individual has to work on themselves and bring their whole person to a relationship. When it comes to relationships, two halves do not make a whole. Two halves actually make a completely toxic relationship.

We are not talking about a man who takes his time to get to know someone. We are talking about the man who has problems attaching emotionally and committing to a woman. The most deceptive aspect about this man is that he often looks great on paper. He may have a successful business or excel in his career. A good woman looks for a man who is dedicated to his work, goal oriented, and committed to success. These are all traits that indicate the potential for a solid, long lasting relationship. Yet a man can be a powerhouse at work, while behaving like an insecure puppy in his personal life. His ego may only be able to handle a mediocre (usually emotionally unstable) female because she has to appear to be weaker than him for him to feel like he is the head of the household.

SCENARIO 1

After Josh's mother passed unexpectedly, he dropped out of school and was subsequently homeless and living in a shelter. He is just getting back on his feet, but he is still struggling to make ends meet. Maria met Josh at the homeless shelter, where she was the manager. They conversed quite a bit while he was at the shelter and developed a really nice friendship. Josh expressed that he thought she was attractive and would like to spend more time with her.

When Josh comes to her place, Maria is impressed with how thoughtful he is. He is usually available in the evenings after work, so he regularly starts bringing Maria dinner and a Red Box movie. They have started having sex and Maria loves the companionship.

On weekends Maria and Josh spend time going to wine tastings, museums and the movies; she pays for all of these outings. When they see a movie in which a mother dies of cancer, Josh becomes very emotional and Maria notices a change in his behavior. Afterward, he is suddenly very distant. Josh now calls less often and their interactions have been reduced to occasional text messages that are very brief. Josh does not seem as interested as he used to be.

Use the space provided on the next page to list the red flags you found in the above scenario.

We were able to identify the following red flags:

1) Josh is still coping with the death of his mother. He is obviously not handling it well since he dropped out of school and was subsequently homeless and living in a shelter. He doesn't appear to have a support system, seems not be seeking therapy, and is avoiding his emotions until they snowball.

2) He is just getting back on his feet, but he is still struggling to make ends meet. Most good men will not want to bring a woman into his life with nothing to offer but challenges. A man should not be okay with a woman taking care of him, unless he is married and lost his job. This is an indication that you may end up with grown boy on your hands.

3) In-home dates are hardly, if ever, a good idea when just meeting someone. Maria should have insisted on some daytime dates before she started letting him come over for dinner and movies. Even if you are trying to work around schedules, there is always time for a daytime date when you are getting to know the person. If not, the man should take himself off of the dating market until he is able to devote the time and effort to growing a relationship. In-home dates simulate a relationship before there is one and can cause confusion, especially when sex becomes a factor.

4) Maria thinks she can fix his problems when what he needs is professional help. Josh was overcome with the emotions sparked by the movie and became distant. This is a situation where he may need grief counseling. His

mother died suddenly, and he is clearly overwhelmed with grief over the loss. This is not the time to put on your Dr. Phil hat and try to help him out of his situation. Women tend to want to fix people. We can also be driven by a challenging situation. Emotionally unavailable men can sometimes make us want to vie harder for their attention, and fight harder not to lose them. But love is when two whole people come together as one. If one is whole and the other is not, the relationship will be lopsided and the other person will become drained, mentally and emotionally.

SCENARIO 2

Dana and Marcel met at a Fall Festival and discovered that they enjoy similar music. They discussed going to an upcoming concert and exchanged numbers.

Phone conversations went well at first, but over time he began talking about random women who he has disdain for, yet he says that he is attracted to them physically and would sleep with if he had the opportunity. When Dana expressed her discomfort with the nature of the discussions, Marcel became visibly angry, but shut down and would not talk about it. When Dana tried to change the subject to the concert, Marcel suddenly became unavailable that weekend. Dana decided to leave and let Marcel cool off.

When Dana got home, she checked Facebook and saw that Marcel posted a status that she believes was passively directed toward her. Dana is thinking that she may need to cut her losses before she spends any more time or energy.

Can you spot the red flags in the above scenario?

Write them in the space provided on the next page.

We spotted these red flags:

1) If a man expresses a disdain for women, he may not have gotten over being previously hurt. It is not a woman's job to fix him. He must be willing to accept love if a relationship is going to be pursued.

2) A man should not be discussing with you who else he would like to have sex with. This is very disrespectful and insulting to say the least. This also shows that he has not totally graduated from the casual sex club. Being emotionally unavailable will cause the primary focus to be on sex because he does not have to connect emotionally to have sex. Don't be fooled into thinking that this man will change overnight by virtue of being involved with you.

3) Any time a man totally avoids conflict although you are being civil, FLAG ON THE PLAY. As emotionally healthy adults, we should be able to have a discussion about something that concerns us in a respectful way. Communication is like oxygen to a relationship; when it is lacking, the relationship cannot survive.

4) Any kind of passive aggressive behavior is a huge red flag for emotional instability and immaturity. Marcel had the opportunity to express himself when Dana was there, but instead he airs his dirty laundry on social media. It's okay to seek outside counsel first, depending on the situation, but he wasn't seeking outside counsel, he was passively attacking her. When the actions are geared towards attacking from a safe distance rather than looking for solutions or addressing the root

causes, then that is the red flag. When you take something to the general public that is almost always the intention (with the exception of the anonymous submissions to the Code Red Flag website).

CHAPTER 7

Mr. Friendly: Oh, She's Just a Friend

In the late 80s, rapper Biz Markie was made famous with his one-hit wonder, *Just a Friend*. The song was comedic in nature telling the story of a woman who was dating a man and referred to her other love interests as friends. Some men have adopted this lingo as well. This makes a man with primarily or only friends of the opposite sex (a majority of whom he has slept with), and everywhere he goes, a woman seems to know him intimately, a CODE RED FLAG.

Disclaimer: This applies to some, not all relationships of the opposite sex. Let's first define a friend. For the purposes of this book, we will say that a friend is one you spend a lot of time talking to, texting, or hanging out with in person. You share intimate details about yourself and your love life. A friend typically knows more about you than an acquaintance. With that said, we are only going to address friends of the opposite sex, as acquaintances are typically acceptable and not a problem until they enter the friend zone. Many (but not all) long standing friends of the opposite sex began as a potential or an actual relationship, but it didn't work out due to a lack of compatibility. Most people won't admit it, but many times one or both of the "friends" are physically attracted to the other.

Men and women are designed to be together intimately. If they are so close, and not together, usually one is not attracted to the other, otherwise it would seem that their closeness would make for an awesome relationship. Whether or not they have been sexually intimate previously, some men will keep a lady "friend" around so that he can leave the possibility of sex open. Most honest women will tell you that any one of their "friends" of the opposite sex would be ready and willing to have sex with her at any given time. That doesn't mean that they would have a relationship, but sex may be a factor. There are instances where there is mutual respect, but these instances are rare.

If a man has to always have a plan B, he is not secure enough in who he is as a man. He is not confident in his abilities to keep a good woman, so he keeps another on the bench, just in case. The problem comes in when he begins to treat the friend like a girlfriend. Getting too emotionally attached can cause both parties to think that there is something real between them. This can lead to doubting the current relationship and focusing on the negatives to convince himself that something is lacking and his mate is slacking. His girlfriend or wife may be doing what she is supposed to do, but he is distracted and his focus is in so many different places that he can't see the "forest for the trees." When the friend on the side gets promoted from the friend zone, there can be disappointment and dissatisfaction after the initial excitement wears off.

An example of this is a man who is either in a committed relationship or married who talks to his "friends" about his relationship problems instead of discussing these issues with his mate or spouse. He may test the water occasionally to see how far he can go. If a committed man begins to discuss his relationship woes with you, we suggest you quickly cut it off and tell him to work it out with his mate and/or a professional conflict specialist. Conversations like this can turn into "what you would do if you were my mate?" These things open doors for too many problems.

Dena's story:

I had a married male classmate in law school with whom I became friendly. We would often have group outings and we shared many of the same friends. Being little Miss Social, I was normally the person who would arrange these group outings.

After finals one year, I emailed him and others to meet up for drinks. The next day, his wife responded to that email asking why her husband and I would be going out for drinks and how often were these types of outings occurring. Although

I was bothered by her confrontational tone in the email, I replied to her with my phone number and she called me. We spoke and I let her know that she need not worry about me and her husband since we were just friends.

After graduation, I was organizing another group outing and invited him. At some time during our dinner, this man, who I thought of as my friend, began playing footsies with me. I mouthed for him to stop several times but he refused. I decided to leave.

On the way back to my hotel, my "friend" calls me asking which hotel I was staying at and what my room number was. I was livid. I told him off and hung up the phone on him. He called back over ten times and I had to turn my ringer off.

The next day, he texted me an apology and blamed his advances on his alcohol consumption. I told him I accepted his apology but no longer felt comfortable being his friend. I have not spoken to him ever since.

SCENARIO 1

Kenya and Greg are engaged to be married. She says they have what appears to be a wonderful relationship. Greg is supportive, loving, and sweet. Recently, Kenya found out that Greg has been contacting his exes via social media and text messages. When confronted, he lied and said they were just friends. Greg only admitted to the truth when she read aloud the messages in front of him. The messages included things like, "I miss you! I love you," and "maybe we can try this again!" She is at a loss on what to do because she feels that Greg is great--when they are together. But as soon as he gets access to his phone or computer, he is back to reaching out to those from his past. Greg has told her that he has not been physically intimate with these women since they have been together but she is not sure how long that will last.

Are there red flags Kenya should be concerned about? Write the in the space provided on the next page.

These are the red flags we believe should raise concern:

1) The fact that Kenya felt the need to snoop into Greg's phone and social media accounts is a red flag. Often times women feel the need to catch their cheating mate red handed. Many women have said that they don't want to walk away from a relationship on just a hunch. But that hunch is often the red flag waving at you. When Kenya began to feel that she could not trust Greg she should have had a conversation with him about what was causing those feelings to arise. The outcome of that conversation and his actions after would have shown her whether she'd be able to trust him. And if she couldn't regain the trust, she needed to be okay with walking away from that relationship since it was

now causing her grief instead of adding to her joy.

2) Once Kenya confronts Greg with what she found while snooping, he responds with a lie. It is our belief that lies beget more lies. As the trust in their relationship is already damaged, his lying compounds the troubles they face. Since he has been caught in a lie, how can Kenya truly believe he has not slept with one of these women during their relationship?

3) The Law of Attraction says that the more one focuses his/her thoughts on something, the more likely one is to attract that into his/her life. Greg is not only focusing his thoughts on these women, he has acted on the thoughts and is contacting them. We have seen this situation

countless times when dealing with men who need a lot of attention from different women. This also happens with men who have a pattern of rushing into relationships. Some men fall hard and fast but lose interest quickly. Greg should not be telling anyone other than his fiancée that he misses her. The phrase, "maybe we can try this again," could only be sexual in nature in Greg's mind. Regardless of what he meant that is definitely a red flag. FLAG ON THE PLAY.

SCENARIO 2

When Mark and Selena met, Mark seemed reluctant to get into a relationship. Selena knew that Mark was a great catch, so she was persistent. Selena helped Mark wherever she saw that he could use some organization. Mark just had a house built and Selena assisted with packing and moving. Shortly after Mark moved in, Selena began spending a lot of time at Mark's house and they decided to move in together to save money.

Selena was not really comfortable with the fact that Mark had so many female friends, but he said that she would have to accept them or not be with him. Selena reluctantly accepted the friendships, but later found out that one of the females that he kept in regular contact with was someone he had previously had sex with. Selena was very uncomfortable with this, but she desperately wanted to be with Mark.

Even though Mark appeared to be very committed, he wanted to maintain these friendships and even "hang out" with his female friends with and without Selena present. Initially, Mark said that he wanted to get married and start a family. Now Mark is saying that he does not need a piece of paper to validate their relationship. Selena wants to be married and start a family.

Are there red flags that need to be worked out before they consider walking down the aisle? Write them in the space provided below.

We identified the following red flags:

1) Mark was reluctant to enter into a relationship, yet Selena was persistent. Selena should not think that she can change Mark by pushing him into a relationship. If he is not ready, there is nothing she can do to make him ready. This kind of behavior reverses the roles, and the woman becomes the pursuer. This is a major turn off for some men, especially if he has told you that he is not ready. This is a set up for Selena being in a position where she is the long-term girlfriend that does not turn into the wife. When a man finds himself in a situation that he did not want to begin with, he may begin to disconnect without letting the woman know in an effort to spare her feelings.

2) If Selena was not comfortable with the fact that Mark had so many lady friends, she should not have accepted it. This is one of the major foundational issues that two people should be in agreement about. Having friends of the opposite sex can open doors for infidelity, or at least the appearance of it. If Selena is not comfortable with it, and just sucks it up, that does not mean that she feels differently. This will be a recurring issue for her. The more she pretends to accept it, and the more Mark interacts with his friends, Selena will build up resentment. This unresolved issue can lead to insecurity and anger that comes out in other areas of the relationship.

3) No woman should be so desperate to be with a man that she is willing to accept what she considers a deal breaker. Mark obviously was

not as concerned about losing her since he told her to basically, "take it or leave it."

4) If a man tells you that he has changed his mind about marriage and children, believe him. Waiting around to see if a man is going to marry you after he has made his intentions clear is pointless. This is why living together is not always the best idea. People become comfortable with the situation, and it begins to feel like something it is not. If a man is not interested in marriage or children and you try to force him, you are setting yourself up for failure.

CHAPTER 8

Mr. Straight No Chaser: I Don't Chase

If a man refuses to pursue a woman, he is likely either insecure or has a football team of prospects chasing him down like he's running the ball straight for the end zone. This guy is likely very physically attractive but very insecure. He keeps himself distracted by multiple women and waits for one to "step up to the plate."

He will ask for a picture of you to put in his phone as your contact pic so that he can see who is who. He is tallying how many times you call and text, to determine who is more interested. He also tallies how many times you offer to cook for him, how good the food is and how clean your house is.

Please believe that you are also in competition for how well you can perform sexually. He may even go so far as to say, "how badly do you want to be Mrs. Jones?" during sex. Your pursuit of him is everything he hopes for.

This type of man does not believe there should be reciprocity in a relationship. He prefers to take advantage of each and any opportunity that comes his way, because he can. Because he is attractive, has an amazing body, a good career and brings home a good salary, he believes that any woman should be happy to be with him and just do what a good woman is supposed to do: submit to him without any question.

He has little interest in your dreams, he does not support what you are passionate about, and he would rather debate others on social media for hours than have a decent conversation with you. When it comes to your needs, he is constantly distracted, but when it comes to his needs, he is fully attentive. He rants and raves if you slip, but cannot and will not hold himself accountable.

When asked what a man should be bringing to the table, he cannot articulate a clear and concise response. He either says "I don't know" or gives a generic answer like, "I love hard and I try."
Both parties have to put in effort and take action to make things work in a relationship. The women pursuing Mr. I Don't Chase are the only ones putting forth any effort. He just sits back and reaps the reward because he believes he is the prize.

Ladies, the dating game is simple. Look at the man's track record. When it comes to dating, you should act like a human resources manager. Do more listening than talking during the "getting to know you " interview phase. Do a background check (a quick Google search should suffice) and ask your friends and associates if they know him. You can also add him on social media to try to get a feel for what he is talking about and how others relate to him. Don't be in a rush to have sex, because great sex has the tendency to cloud judgment.

This man has a warped view of relationships. Not only does he believe that he does not have to pursue a woman, but he believes that women are lazy, don't know how to take care of a man, and need to "woman up."

A man like this likes to be flashy and pretend like he has a lot going for him so that he can feel better about himself. His career, social organizations, and tons of women chasing him makes him who he is. Strip the degrees, career, and attention away and he may sink into a depressive state. All in all, a man and a woman need to be secure in themselves outside of material and tangible things prior to getting into a relationship.

SCENARIO 1

Sara met Kevin at her community health club. They realized that they had a lot in common. They both liked to cook healthy foods and exercise, just to name a few things. Since they only live a couple of blocks from each other, they exchanged numbers and parted ways.

On subsequent visits to the health club, Kevin would ask Sara why she has not called him yet. Each time they saw each other out, either at the grocery store or the local sports bar, Kevin acted very interested. He regularly talked about taking her out and once he even told Sara that he was going to take her out for Mexican the following day. Yet Sara received no call and continued to not hear from Kevin. Sara thinks that Kevin may just be nervous about reaching out to her, so she is considering calling him.

Are there red flags that Sara's missing? Write them in the space provided on the next page.

We think Sara has missed the following red flags:

1) A man who is really interested and available, emotionally or otherwise, he will not hesitate to call. If a man acts interested in person, but refuses to call, he is not nervous; he expects a woman to chase him. If two people have expressed mutual interest and exchanged numbers, it is fine for a woman to call, however she should not be the only one putting in all of the effort.

2) If a man repeatedly talks about doing something, but does not follow through, he is not reliable. You must throw a FLAG ON THE PLAY.

SCENARIO 2

Marla and John work in the same office building, but for different companies. They were instantly attracted to each other and began chatting when they met in the building cafeteria one morning. John asked Marla for her number so that they could "hang out sometime," and they exchanged numbers. Marla was excited about the possibility of dating someone because she had gotten to a point where she was comfortable with being single.

Marla found herself giving her number to John a couple of times because he would get her number and not use it, claiming that he lost it. After the third time, Marla decided to take the initiative and contact John. They went out a couple of times, but only after Marla suggested that they catch a movie and a bite to eat. They went Dutch, which was not a problem for

Marla. However, when John initiated contact with her, he asked to come to her house so that she could cook for him. Marla did not feel that she knew John well enough to invite him into her home, so she repeatedly declined. Marla decided to give John a chance to step up and she stopped contacting him.

The other day he sent her a message via social media, upset because she stopped contacting him. Marla asked John why he could not contact her, and he said that if she was interested she would have contacted him because he does not chase.   Marla felt that perhaps John getting upset was his way of showing her that he is interested.

What red flags have Marla missed? Write them in the space provided on the next page.

We found the following red flags:

1) Marla should not have needed to give him her number several times if he was truly interested. Greg being that preoccupied or forgetful shows he may not be in a position to put effort into developing a relationship.

2) Greg knew that Marla was interested but still did not initiate contact. If he was truly interested in getting to know her, Marla would not have to be the one contacting him each time they talk, nor would she be the only one suggesting that they go out and setting it up. Greg is obviously used to sitting back and letting the woman put in all of the work. It is time to teach Greg that a quality woman who is bringing something to the table deserves a quality man who is doing the

same. Relationships are not designed for lazy people. FLAG ON THE PLAY

3) It seems Marla is a modern woman. She is comfortable being single, which suggests she's put the work into herself to become whole. She's okay going Dutch, showing she takes care of her finances. She's clearly looking for a partner, not a caretaker, while Greg, who is trying to evaluate her cooking skills, may be looking for a servant. There's nothing wrong with a woman who wants to stay at home and have a "traditional" relationship, but it doesn't sound like Marla is this kind of woman. That may be a fundamental mismatch that will not be resolved.

CHAPTER 9

Mr. Bartender: The Unquenchable Thirst Monster

This is the kind of man that is so overly assertive--aka thirsty--that he might as well chill behind the bar and serve himself. We are of the opinion that the term 'thirsty' has damaged the courting experience and should be left in 2013 because so many people are overly concerned with being seen as acting thirsty that they sacrifice the expression of general interest. Most illustrations of interest are reasonable when balance is incorporated.

Mr. Bartender can be used to describe a man who sacrifices his self-dignity for sex/relationship and/or sucks one woman dry to satisfy his thirst. Or he may be a man with an insatiable appetite who needs a plethora of women to suck the life out of. Both of these men need either sex or a relationship to fill a void.

Mr. Bartender is often arrogant yet insecure, typically a womanizer. A man with an insatiable appetite for women, he could have a great woman who is putting in 110% and has a lifetime supply of Gatorade to pour down his throat daily, but he will still remain parched. The attention-seeking variety will use social media as his platform. He needs "likes" and "supporters" to make him feel better about himself. He is often very flashy, charismatic, and he has an image that he must uphold no matter how bad things get in life. He will probably spend a lot of time talking about himself and his accomplishments because that is what validates him (other than women).

There are men who have a great front that disguises the thirst. They come across as an alpha male who appears to know what he wants and brags about being able to get what he wants. This is the guy who uses social media as a platform for advertising himself because he knows that it will get him the sex he desires, satisfying his thirst only momentarily.

On the flip side, there is the man who wears his insecurity on his sleeve. He will sacrifice his masculinity and conform his personality/beliefs to the woman he is with in an effort to maintain the relationship. This man will fall hard and fast for the first woman who shows him any sort of attention without really getting to know her. This man is so desperate for any kind of relationship, that simply a smile and a good morning will cause him to instantly think that the woman wants him, thus he pounces. He may be over the top with texts, phone calls, instant messages, e-mails compliments, and will say things like, "you are so far out of my league that I really don't deserve you."

There is a difference between a confident man who goes after what he wants by showing interest and a man who will stop his entire life for a love interest. If a man cannot say no to a woman, no matter how outrageous the request, he needs some water.

This type of man is actually over-compensating for his inability, real or perceived, to maintain a relationship by just being himself. This is the guy who will ditch his favorite football team, leave his church, and alter his life to revolve around a woman. There are some controlling women who would like this scenario initially. However, after a while the challenge of being able to control a man is gone and he will get played to the left. In a healthy relationship, each individual maintains their identity, while being in agreement about some fundamental issues (i.e. sex, money, children and religion). A healthy couple will agree to disagree on some things and love each other for the differences they have.

Most women want a driven man who has an innovative spirit and "hustle" in his heart. They want a trend setter and a go getter, not a follower who needs his woman to tell him his opinion before he can make any decision for the advancement of the team.

This is not to say that a woman's opinion is not needed, wanted or valued. However, if your man has to make a quick decision, during an emergency for instance, he should be able to do that. Most women find a sense of protection in a man who can stand on his own two feet. As the saying goes, "if you won't stand for something, you will fall for anything." If a man is willing to "wait for you" while you decide whether or not you are going to stay in your current relationship, that is not chivalrous. It's thirsty.

Don't be mistaken, men who love and care for the woman they love should be celebrated. There is nothing sexier than a man who can be a pitbull out in the world and nothing but a gentleman at home with his woman. A gentleman knows that the woman has the power in the relationship even though he may be the head. He would only choose a queen who uses that power to build him up and not tear him down. And he knows he doesn't have to play Mr. Bartender to attract such a woman.

SCENARIO 1

Kate met Jeff online. Jeff distinguished himself from other suitors because he was so persistent and he let his intentions be known. On their first date, Jeff asked Kate to date him exclusively. Kate was excited about this because she was taught that a man should know what he wants and go after it. She was also taught that if a man wants her, he will make it very clear. Kate agreed and they took a picture together.

The next day Jeff changed his social media profile pictures to the picture they had taken together, and he changed his relationship status to "in a relationship." Many people began to comment on the status change and many of the comments were, "boy, you change women like you change your boxers" and "you keep a woman on the bench, don't you?"

Within the next week, Jeff begins talking about marriage and taking Kate to New Jersey to meet his family. Kate is concerned that things are moving way too fast.

Are there red flags she should be concerned with? Write them in the space provided on the next page.

The red flags we found were:

1) A man who is serious about finding a quality woman will take his time in getting to know her before asking her to be exclusive. A mature man who is dating with a purpose wants to know that the woman he is getting involved with has the potential to be a good wife and mother. A first date is way too early.

2) It is also not wise to expose a relationship on social media before you really get to know each other. Many men won't put their business on social media until there's an engagement. This opens the relationship up to attack before it can get started. Not everyone wants to see others happy, especially if they are not happy. Getting to know each other in private, while establishing

a foundation, is key. There is a difference between hiding a relationship and keeping it private.

3) If people are indicating that a man has been in a series of short-lived relationships, and he is rushing into a relationship with you, this is a pattern of his. It is not a good sign when someone does not think things through and makes an impulsive decision based on emotion. Considering the fact that Jeff not only has short lived relationships, but also puts all of them on social media, he deserves a FLAG ON HIS PLAY.

4) Once a man has gotten to know you, and knows that he can see himself with you long-term, that is a beautiful thing. Talking about marriage in general within a week is fine, but talking about marrying *you* in a week deserves a FLAG ON

THE PLAY. Marriage is a serious thing and should not be taken lightly. Both people need to determine if they are in agreement about the things in life that are most important to them and could potentially affect future children.

Most married people say that they never totally know their spouse because, as life goes on, different situations may come up that can bring out new sides of people, both good and bad. One needs to be prepared for the fact that the person they choose to be with can stay the same, improve or get worse.

When you make that step toward marriage, you have to make up in your mind that you are going to accept someone as they are, for better and for worse. That will never happen in a week.

SCENARIO 2

Leslie has been dating Rod for a few weeks. Recently, her girlfriends invited her for a ladies' night out on the town. When she tells Rod her plans he asked if he could accompany her. Leslie explains that it will just be the ladies and Rod seems to accept that.

On the night she goes out, Rod calls Leslie over 20 times that evening. When she answers and he hears men in the background he quickly accuses her of cheating and lying to him that it would only be the ladies on the excursion.

At the end of the night when Leslie gets home Rod is sitting on her porch. Leslie thinks that a little jealousy is cute and shows that Rod really cares for her. But her friends call him thirsty and crazy.

Should Leslie be concerned?   Identify the red flags

that should raise her concerns in the space provided

on the next page.

Here are the red flags we identified:

1) Rod did not want Leslie to go on the ladies' night outing without him. In a relationship, both parties need to have a social life outside of the relationship. This does not mean that someone acting single when they are out with friends is okay. It means that there should be healthy interactions with people of the same sex. You both need time apart to keep the relationship fresh. Without that, one or both people will begin to feel smothered.

2) Rod was being insecure by calling Leslie over 20 times on a night when he knew she had plans to go out with her girlfriends. His unrelenting need for her attention throughout the night puts him in the thirsty category.

3) Rod seems to have stalker tendencies since he was waiting on Leslie's steps when she arrived home. How long had he been sitting there? He should have taken this opportunity to go out with his friends while she enjoyed hers. Instead, he obsessed over her moves all night and then, to make sure she came home alone, he sat waiting for her. This screams Code Red Flag, Flag OnThe Play!

CHAPTER 10

Mr. Keep It On the Down Low

Mr. Keep It On the Down Low is a man with something to hide. Things may seem great when the two of you are together, but somehow you never see or learn anything else about his life. When you see him, it's either at your place or the two of you go out of town. He won't disclose basic personal information, such as where he lives or works, and he is stealthy about his phone.

Ladies, we all know a Mr. Down Low. However, we women have gotten so used to his ways that sometimes we let paranoia take over and we lose perspective on the difference between down low behavior and genuine privacy. It is great to be able to identify red flags, but keep things in perspective.

When we dig too much, we may see things that aren't really there.

Mandee's Story

I was with a rather reserved man who was not a good communicator, but his actions said a lot about who he was. He was very dependable and was always ready and willing to do something for someone else, especially me. I met several of his friends and the majority of his family at a large family gathering. I was always welcome at family events and there were no restrictions on where he and I could go out (day or night). I was welcome in his residence from day one and I always felt that I could pop over when I wanted to.

Because he had a hard time communicating, when I would occasionally ask him questions about our relationship, he would clam up and not want to talk about it, or he'd give me short quick answers. Many times I was left to make assumptions and figure things out on my own.   It was a huge mistake for both of us.

My insecurity did not allow me to distinguish "hiding" something and keeping something private. Social media should have been the least of my concern, but I could not understand how he could put family pictures and personal information on Facebook, yet keep our relationship guarded.

He would screen the posts that he was tagged in. I was never in any pictures posted and was never tagged in any "check-ins" at places where we went together. I was used to men who were proud to change their relationship status, and couldn't wait to post pictures of us, so this made me very suspicious. Because of my suspicion about what he was doing, everything that happened was questionable.

The straw that broke the camel's back was when his phone dialed me and he didn't know it. I heard him having a conversation with a female. The conversation appeared to be innocent, but I could not get over the fact that he was alone with a female at 10pm. When I had an opportunity to speak with him about it, he became silent and had very little to say.

This poor communication is what led to the demise of the relationship. He could have been a more effective communicator and more emotionally available and I could have stopped being insecure and assuming the worst.

Often, time will reveal the answers to the questions you may have, so asking less questions does not indicate weakness or being gullible. Trust is the foundation of a solid relationship, and sometimes trust takes having a little faith in your partner.

Some men compartmentalize different aspects of their lives, whether it be women, work, organizational membership or male friends. Occasionally men will not mix a love interest with their social life because they know what their friends would say about you when you are not around (possibly sexual in nature). Some good men truly want to keep their personal life private.

Family and children do not change, but relationships do. Even if a man puts family pictures and events on Facebook or Instagram, that doesn't mean that he will put his relationship status out there. A good man will want to give the relationship time to grow, so that the two of you can get to know each other without outside distractions.

Most people have hundreds of Facebook friends, but only know 10% of those people and may only communicate with 5% on a regular basis. The embarrassment of having to change your relationship status from in a relationship to single is unnecessary. Once he puts it on social media, there may be a lot of questions, people keeping tabs on the relationship, and frankly some women and men are turned on when there is more of a challenge to be with someone. Too many outsiders in your relationship is a problem. Think of a relationship as a "ship." If there are a ton of people in your boat and not everyone is rowing, you may sink.

While it is one thing to not want to broadcast your relationship, denying you are in one, as Mr. Down Low would do is a CODE RED FLAG. If you get engaged, or (even worse) married, and your man does not want to change his relationship status or tell his family, that is a CODE RED FLAG. Do not allow a man to use privacy as an excuse to keep your relationship on the down low. Meeting the family and friends is not always an indication that you are the only one because some family and friends will cover for a trifling man.

However, a good man is very selective about who he introduces his family to, especially his mother. Now, if you can't go certain places with him, he only wants to go out of town, or he only takes you to drive through restaurants, COD RED FLAG.

If the man you are seeing can only come over late at night, and the only movies you see together are bootleg or Red Box, CODE RED FLAG. If you don't know where he lives and/or have never been to his house after dating for a while, CODE RED FLAG. If he ignores excessive phone calls while he is with you, and/or constantly hides his phone, CODE RED FLAG. During the "getting to know you" phase, I would not expect for a man to cut off all ties with all other women. Once he has made a commitment to being with you exclusively, he should being putting females from the past on notice.

SCENARIO 1

Michelle wasn't feeling it, but her girls begged her to go out. She hasn't been feeling very pretty since she stopped seeing Mike. She decided that she was going to step out in her tightest, sexiest outfit. When she and her girls arrived at the club, she couldn't get out of the car before men started saying things to her about how sexy she looked.

Once inside, a couple of drunks were quite disrespectful. A quiet, handsome man stepped out of the darkness and gently leaned in to assure her that she was none of the names that the man was calling her. His name was Jay and he bought Michelle a drink. They conversed for a while and instantly hit it off. They exchanged numbers and Jay texted Michelle to make sure that she got home safely.

They communicated over the next few weeks, mostly via text. It would occasionally take him an entire day to respond to a call of text. Jay traveled a lot for work, and he began inviting her to go with him. Michelle was impressed by this. Jay told Michelle that he could not disclose exactly what he did because he had a top secret job with the government. He also used that as the excuse as to why he had two phones that he was constantly on. Jay did a lot of texting, but Michelle chalked it up to him handling business.

While Jay was fine with taking Michelle on trips, she was never invited to meet his co-workers and, after six months of dating, she was not invited to a family gathering at Six Flags theme park. When they travel together, Jay seems to be into Michelle, but when they return home she feels like a complete stranger.

Should she maintain the relationship? Identify the red flags in this scenario in the space provided on the next page.

Here are the red flags we identified:

1) Michelle hadn't been feeling very pretty since she stopped seeing Mike. A woman's confidence must come from within. If we depend on another flawed human being to determine how we feel about ourselves, we will be constantly disappointed and insecure. This is not the state that you want to be in when going out. A man who preys on women with low self-esteem will be able to determine this from a mile away. Based on how Michelle was dressed, she was giving off the vibe that any attention (even negative or degrading attention) is better than no attention. When a woman is willing to accept any kind of attention, men know that she is willing to accept most anything that they dish out. They bank on the fact that she will accept

whatever time they give, no matter how minuscule, and whatever excuses they give, no matter how many omissions or blatant lies.

2) They communicated for weeks, mostly via text. It would occasionally take Jay an entire day to respond to a call or text. Someone who constantly looks at their phone while you are around, but takes days to respond is a CODE RED FLAG. In this technology driven age, texting is acceptable, but if that is the primary means of communication when you are trying to get to know someone, CODE RED FLAG. Excessive texting could mean that he cannot reveal to people around him that he is talking to you, or that he is not emotionally available enough for a serious relationship.

3) Jay was fine with taking Michelle on trips, but she was never invited to meet his co-workers and, after six months of dating, nor was she invited to a family gathering at Six Flags theme park. Everyone is not ready to be married after six months, but most people who are ready to settle down know if they want something long term with the person they have been dating exclusively for six months. If he has not said anything about the future with you in it, and has not introduced you to his family and friends, CODE RED FLAG. Either he can't reveal you to these people because of his relationship status (married or in a serious relationship), or you are not the one.

4) When they travel together, Jay seems to be into Michelle, but when they return home she feels like a complete stranger. Again, this is an

indication that Jay lives with a spouse or a significant other. If he travels a lot for work, and his spouse or significant other trusts him, he can get away with living a separate life on the road.

SCENARIO 2

Jill and Seth have been dating for about a year and she feels that he is perfect for her. Seth can't see himself without her. She has met his family, friends and they have experienced a lot of life together. Their relationship has occasionally been rocky because Jill has an overwhelming need to fix everything with Seth at the exact moment it happens instead of just giving him space and time to figure things out. This bothers him because he feels that he has proven himself to have sound decision-making skills and he wants to be the head of his household.

He loves getting Jill's input because she is very intelligent and business savvy. However, if she feels that there is even a minor problem that she cannot fix right then, she will get anxious and occasionally have a panic attack. She says that it is because she cares so much, but it makes Seth have pause. Jill has great attributes that he feels as though he can't live without, but her need for control is creating a conflict.

Jill pressured Seth to propose and now that they have gotten engaged, Seth refuses to let the status change be known and social media and even his family. Jill is devastated.

Use the space provided on the next page to identify the red flags in this scenario.

Here are the red flags we identified:

1) Jill is more of a red flag than Seth in this scenario. As the saying goes, Rome was not built in a day. Jill should not have the expectation that she can fix everything that she feels is wrong at the exact moment it happens. When a woman chooses a man to be the head of her household, she needs to allow him to do just that. If you are not confident with his abilities to make decisions, then you should not be with him.

2) Getting anxious and actually having panic attacks is indicative of a deeply rooted issue that may only improve with professional help. Another flawed human being can only compliment your stability. He cannot keep you

in a state of happiness and security at all times. Just as a man is expected to come into a relationship with a certain level of maturity and emotional stability, the same is expected of a woman. If you display this kind of behavior over minor problems, he will wonder what your response will be to bigger issues, like the pressure of having children and maintaining a household.

3) If a man is to find a wife, let him choose to marry you in his own time. If his time frame seems to be too long for you, then move on. Seth's behavior in regard to keeping the engagement a secret is a red flag, however he is having second thoughts for good reason. He should be mature enough to not allow himself to be pressured into something he does not want to do, but he is clearly in love with Jill and does

not want to hurt or disappoint her. This needs

to be a wake-up call for Jill to get herself

together.

CONCLUSION

As women, we have the power to set the tone in our relationships. You've heard the old adages, "a man will only do to you what you allow," and, "what you allow will continue." When you allow men to disrespect you, you will constantly attract disrespectful men.

Throughout this book we have illustrated red flags that occur while dating and during relationships. We don't doubt that many of you were able to recognize these red flags immediately. That is good. However, if a healthy relationship is what you desire, you must learn to recognize these red flags when it comes to your relationships just as easily. Don't be blinded by lust and infatuation. Those are only hurdles along the journey to finding your Mr. Right.

Being a queen not only means knowing how to take care of a man, it also requires that you know how to take care of yourself in the absence of a man. When we fall for the many Mr. Wrongs that we will inevitably meet during our journey through life, we are telling God and the universe we are not yet prepared for the one who is meant for us.

When we ignore red flags and accept a man's nonsense, we are complicit in hurting generations of families. A woman has the ability to encourage a man to greatness or destruction. As women we need to help our men become kings. We can start doing that by not allowing peasant-like behavior in our relationships.

Don't beat yourself up for making past mistakes, this book is designed to help you identify areas for improvement. Lost love was meant to teach you, not hurt you, so be better not bitter. With the ability to identify red flags, you will find there will be times when you have to let a man go. This is for his own good as well as your sanity. If losing a good woman causes him to change his game for the next woman because you wouldn't put up with it, so be it and thanks for taking one for the team. You have just paid it forward and you will reap your blessing in your due time. Every man is not a good man for you. If you are no longer with someone, it is for a reason.

THE END

ABOUT THE AUTHOR

REID, ESQ.

Founder and President of Code Red Flag, Dena Reid is a legally trained Conflict Mediator specializing in family and domestic disputes. Ms. Reid holds a Bachelor's of Science from Cornell University as well as a Juris Doctorate from Georgetown University Law Center. Additionally, Ms. Reid holds numerous certifications in mediation and arbitration from the Scheinman Institute on Conflict Resolution. Ms. Reid has also worked as Commissioner of Mediation for the Federal Mediation & Conciliation Service. She uses her training and experience to help families and couples deal with conflict in a productive and mutually beneficial manner.

At 34 years old, Ms. Reid is single and childless. She says she is attempting to be more like the biblical character Ruth as she strives to grow her empire while waiting on her Boaz to find her. She hopes to one day be an illustration of a woman who has balanced work and life with a successful career, loving husband, and family. Until that day she will continue to "Mogul Up."